The Sugarless Baking Book

THE SUGARLESS BAKING BOOK

The Natural Way to Prepare
America's Favorite Breads,
Pies, Cakes, Puddings and Desserts

Patricia Mayo

Illustrated by Richard Spencer

Autumn  Press

Published by **Autumn ❧ Press, Inc.**
with editorial offices at
25 Dwight Street
Brookline, Massachusetts 02146

Distributed in the United States
by Random House, Inc., and in
Canada by Random House of Canada, Ltd.
Copyright © 1979 by Patricia Mayo
All rights reserved.

Library of Congress Catalog Card Number: 79-51818
ISBN: 0-394-73768-7
Printed in the United States of America
Typeset at dnh, Cambridge, Massachusetts
Illustrated by Richard Spencer

Book design and typography by Beverly Stiskin

TO OUR HEALTH

TABLE OF CONTENTS

Unyeasted Breads

Yeasted Breads

Acknowledgments

I wish to thank my family for their encouragement and support. I especially thank my husband, Doug, for taste-testing all of my experiments; and my mother, Helen H. Terris, for believing in me (and letting me use her typewriter!). I also need to thank Lynda LeMole and Deborah Balmuth for their thoughtful editorial advice and thanks to Beverly Stiskin and Nahum Stiskin for all of their talents used in making this a beautiful book.

Using Natural Ingredients

Why Use Natural Ingredients?

Almost everyone has heard about de-natured foods: these are refined foods, such as white flour, white sugar, and saturated fats that have had most of their nutrients removed during processing and packaging. While the refining process increases the shelf-life of various foods (the amount of time a product can sit on the shelf and not spoil), it decreases the nutritive value of these foods. In order to put nutrients back into your diet, you may want to use more unprocessed, natural ingredients in your food preparation.

This cookbook will provide the beginner with a fundamental knowledge of some of these ingredients and their use in baking, as well as offer a starting point for the cook who is seeking a more healthful diet. The recipes call for whole grain flours, natural liquid sweeteners, and liquid vegetable or seed oils. When you become acquainted with the flavors of whole grain flours or honey, you will begin to prefer them to the taste of white flour or sugar. The use of these ingredients can be a big step in the direction of more healthful eating, and the food that you prepare with them will be nutritious and satisfying.

Basic Ingredients

Whole Grain Flours supply the B vitamins and fibre, two important nutrients removed from white flour during the milling process. When white flour is milled, the wheat bran and wheat germ are removed from the ground grain. These two parts of the grain contain 11 of the B vitamins found in wheat. Fibre, which is believed to prevent many intestinal disorders, is concentrated in the wheat bran. White flour has only 7–8% of the fibre found in whole wheat flour.

Liquid Sweeteners include honey, maple syrup, and molasses. Refined sugar, which includes brown sugar and so-called "raw" sugar, is almost 100% sucrose. When ingested, white sugar requires drastic response on the part of the pancreas and the adrenal glands. Natural sweeteners contain lower percentages of sugar which are less of a jolt to the hormonal system. Refined sugar requires that minerals and vitamins be withdrawn from the body's stores in order for it to be digested and metabolized. Natural sweeteners contain many of the minerals and enzymes necessary for their digestion.

Liquid Vegetable and Seed Oils provide essential fatty acids to the body. Two of these essential acids, linoleic and linolenic, are refined out of most processed fats. Corn and soybean oil contain 35–70% linoleic acid and safflower oil contains 85–90%. Another fatty substance necessary to the body, lecithin, is lost when oil is refined or hydrogenated (as in shortenings or margarine). Lecithin is a source of two B vitamins, cholin and inositol. Vitamin E, also lost in the refining process, is the vitamin that preserves the freshness of natural oils.

By changing from white flour to whole grain flour, from sugar to liquid sweeteners, and from refined or hydrogenated fats to liquid oils, you will restore many valuable nutrients to your diet.

Where to Obtain Natural Ingredients

Some supermarkets now have natural foods sections which might be the most convenient way to get acquainted with some of these whole foods. Health food stores are growing quickly and it is likely that there is one nearby. The staff in these stores is usually knowledgeable and willing to answer any of your questions. Food co-ops are another source of natural foods. They can be located through your town office, community center or welfare office. Not all co-ops have made the change to whole foods, but some have and this is the most economical way to buy.

What's Available

Whole Grain Flours

Whole Wheat Flour is the standard baking flour. It may be ground from spring or winter wheat and is used in breads and some pastries.

Whole Wheat Pastry Flour is ground from soft wheat and used for a finer-textured result, as in cakes and pies.

Rye flour provides a distinctive flavor and a heavier texture.

There are many other flours available such as soy, rice, oatmeal and triticale flours. However, those listed are used most often. Flour is usually sold by the pound and can be purchased boxed, bagged or in bulk. Pre-packaged flour, whether in boxes or bags, is likely to be less fresh than bulk flour that you measure and package yourself, such as in a health food store or food co-op. However, packaged flour is easier for stores to handle and for this reason may be more readily available. Whole grain flours are available frozen and freshly ground. When thawed, frozen flour loses its freshness more quickly than freshly ground or pre-packaged flours. In some places, however, it may be all that is available. Some health food stores and co-ops have their own grinders. The grinding may take some extra time, but provides the lightest, freshest flour. If you have your own grinder, you can purchase whole grain wheat and grind it in small amounts as needed. "Stone-ground" flour is ground at a lower speed which causes less heat, resulting in less damage to the nutrients.

Liquid Sweeteners

Honey should be pure. Some honey has cane or corn syrup added so be sure to read the label before buying. Clover or wildflower honey is light-colored and light-flavored. It is preferable to the darker honeys for baking. The darker honeys are rich in minerals, but have strong distinctive flavors, not suitable to the recipes in this book. Honey is sold by the pound. Buy a small amount, 2 to 5 pounds, in order to get acquainted with this new flavor. Later you may want to invest in a larger quantity, such as 60 pounds, available from apiaries or through health food stores and co-ops. This is usually the most inexpensive way to buy.

Maple Syrup sold in supermarkets is usually "blended" syrup, made with cane or corn syrups added. Read the labels to make sure that you are getting pure maple syrup. Maple syrup has a lighter flavor than honey and is particularly desirable in recipes such as Tapioca Pudding or Vanilla Cookies. It is interchangeable with honey in any of the recipes. Use the same amount of syrup as listed for honey.

Unsulphured Molasses is recommended for use in many of the recipes. It is the juice of the sugar cane, extracted for its own sake and containing many of the nutrients discarded in the refining of sugar. Sulphured molasses is a by-product of the sugar refining process and contains sulphur, used in that process. Molasses has a strong flavor, just right for Indian Pudding or Gingerbread Men.

Liquid Oils

Safflower, Sesame, and Sunflower oils are light-flavored and light-colored. Any of the three is suitable for the recipes.

Corn oil has a flavor similar to butter. It is a good substitute when the distinctive flavor of butter is desired.

Soy oil has a strong soy flavor and is used in other types of cooking more than in baking.

These oils are sold in pint and quart jars. Some stores offer oil in bulk, where you bring your own jar and fill it to the amount desired. As with other bulk products, this is often the least expensive way to buy. Buy small amounts often, as it has a short shelf-life. Store in a cool, dark place and/or in dark bottles.

How To Use Natural Ingredients

Whole Grain Flours should not be sifted unless specified in the recipe. Sifting removes some of the food value but gives a lighter texture desired for cakes and pie crust. The amount of flour listed in any recipe may not be exact, as it depends on factors such as humidity and where or how the flour was ground. When preparing any recipe, add the flour in small amounts. The amount may vary up to ½ cup either way, but most of the recipes include a description of the finished batter or dough for determining when you have added enough flour. If you wish to substitute bread flour for pastry flour, either use less flour or add more liquid to the recipe to attain the desired texture. Bread flour makes drier, firmer baked goods. Be sure to rinse or soak all of the bowls and utensils immediately after use because whole grain dough becomes very hard when dry and will require much soaking and scrubbing to remove.

Liquid Sweeteners can be messy. Wipe up any spills or drips with a hot, wet dish cloth. When pouring sticky sweeteners, you can cut the flow by tipping the jar up and giving it a twist. This also helps prevent drips. Measure liquid sweeteners for any recipe after measuring the liquid oil; the oil coats the sides of the measuring cup so the sweetener will slip right out of the measuring cup into the bowl. Honey, syrup and molasses all wash off easily with hot water and soap.

Liquid Oils are much easier to handle than shortening. Measure the desired amount in a liquid measuring cup. When added to other ingredients, the liquid oil stirs in easily and thoroughly. Hot water and soap will clean off oil on utensils or counters.

Most of the recipes call for an oiled pan. To oil, pour a small amount onto the pan or baking sheet; a dot the size of a quarter should be adequate. Use a large piece of waxed paper folded into several thicknesses to spread the oil evenly over bottom and sides of the pan. When oiling baking sheets, there is no need for additional oil between batches of cookies on the sheet—just redistribute the oil already on the sheet. To make cakes easy to remove, lightly dust the sides and bottom of the pan with flour after oiling. To insure easy removal of breads, oil the pan and sprinkle with corn meal. Carefully remove baked goods from the pan after baking. Loosen cakes and breads from the pans by gently running a sharp knife around the edge of the pan. Hot, soapy water will remove any oil from the pans after baking.

Liquid Lecithin also may be used to oil pans. Lecithin is a fatty substance, rich in B vitamins, found in liver, yeast, wheat germ and egg yolk. The liquid form, available in health food stores, is extracted from soy oil. As with any purchase, read the label to be sure you are purchasing only pure extract, with no chemical additives used during processing.

A thin coating of liquid lecithin, applied to your baking pans, will prevent *anything* from sticking. A gentle loosening, and the baked goods slide right out. It may seem expensive but a small amount goes a long way. Lecithin is difficult to spread because it is so thick. The easiest way is to heat the baking pan or sheet before applying the lecithin. Place the pan on the top of the stove while the oven is preheating. When the batter has been prepared, pour a thin stream of lecithin over the bottom of the warm cookie sheet or baking pan. Take a large sheet of waxed paper and fold it into several thicknesses. Cover your fingers with the waxed paper and spread the lecithin evenly over bottom and sides of the pan. Use lecithin sparingly for it does have a flavor and too much on the pan will leave a slight taste. When greasing cookie sheets, there is no need for additional lecithin between batches of cookies on the sheet, just redistribute the lecithin already on the sheet. Hot, soapy water will remove lecithin after baking.

How To Store Natural Ingredients

Whole Grain Flours can spoil over a period of time and with exposure to oxygen. However, properly stored, whole grain flour will stay fresh for up to three months. At first, buy a small amount (5 pounds) and see how long it takes to use it up. Then buy to suit your needs so that you will always have fresh flour. Store the flour in airtight containers, such as plastic bags or boxes, in a cool, dry place. The refrigerator is about the best place to insure the freshness of whole grain flours. If you have your own grinder, be sure to store the grain in a cool, dry place, away from insects or rodents. A clean metal or plastic garbage can lined with a large plastic bag is a good storage bin. Pour in the grain, close the bag, and cover the can. You may want to put a heavy rock on the can cover for extra protection.

Liquid Sweeteners must be stored in airtight jars or tins because they evaporate when exposed to the air. They do not need to be refrigerated and will last indefinitely. Edible honey has been found in Egyptian tombs over 3,000 years old. Honey and maple syrup can harden, called "sugaring." However, this does not mean the sweetener is spoiled. It can be reliquified by placing the jar in a pan of warm water and heating slowly over low heat. Do not heat the honey over 115°F. as high temperatures will destroy the enzymes in it.

Maple syrup may form a mold over the surface but this does not spoil the syrup. Simply scrape the mold off and reliquify the syrup to restore its original flavor and consistency. Store molasses in a cool, dry place in an airtight container. It does not harden or "sugar." You may find that you use less of this sweetener and therefore need not keep as much on hand.

Liquid Oils can turn rancid. They must be refrigerated after opening. Kept cold in airtight jars, these oils can last several months. Buying in small amounts more often will insure fresh oil.

Before putting any of the natural ingredients away for storage, label the container with the date of purchase.

Storing Baked Goods

No preservatives are used in baking with natural ingredients, so the baked goods will become moldy and lose freshness if kept for any length of time. Be sure to cool the baked goods completely before storing in airtight containers because any condensation on the inside of a plastic bag from warm food will hasten the growth of mold. If the food is to be eaten immediately, it need not be refrigerated. But if it is to be kept for several days, store it in the refrigerator. To freeze the food for later use, cool the food and wrap well. When thawed, store it in the refrigerator. Foods that have been frozen and thawed lose their freshness more quickly than foods that have not been frozen. Baked goods will last in the freezer for up to one year, although for flavor it is preferable to use them within 4 to 6 months. Before freezing, mark each package with the date of preparation.

Other Natural Ingredients

Here is a list of the other natural ingredients called for in these recipes. All of these ingredients are available in health food stores.

Arrowroot flour: a natural thickener used instead of cornstarch

Baking powder: tartrate baking powder made without aluminum

Baking soda: bicarbonate of soda

Bran flakes: bran of the wheat grain; store in the refrigerator

Brown rice: whole grain rice

Canned fruits: look for fruits that have been canned without sugar added

Caraway seeds: used in rye bread

Carob chips: a substitute for chocolate chips, made with less sugar

Carob powder: made from the edible seed pod of the carob tree, a substitute for chocolate, containing no caffeine. Buy "roasted" carob powder for a richer taste, or roast it yourself.

Coconut: unsweetened, shredded coconut

Corn meal: coarsely ground corn

Dates: organically grown, unsulphured dates. Sulphur is added to many dried fruits as a preservative; try to avoid these.

Date sugar: ground, dried dates

Figs: organically grown, unsulphured figs

Graham crackers: honey-sweetened graham crackers are available

Ice cream: there are several brands of ice cream made with honey rather than sugar

Peanut butter: freshly-ground, unhydrogenated peanut butter is the most nutritious. Chunky-style, salted peanut butter is used in these recipes. It will separate during storage; blend well before each use.

Raisins: unsulphured raisins

Rolled oats: organically grown oats. The long-cooking variety (15 minutes) is used in these recipes.

Sea salt: salt evaporated from sea water, containing none of the chemicals added to commercial salts

Sesame seeds: store in the refrigerator

Spices: the measurements listed are for dry, ground spices. Some spices are available whole, to be freshly ground as needed.

Tapioca: thickener used in puddings and pies

Vanilla: pure vanilla extract, not imitation vanilla flavoring

Walnuts: organically grown walnuts are available shelled and unshelled. Store all shelled nuts in the refrigerator.

Wheat germ: germ of the wheat grain; store in the refrigerator

Yeast: dry yeast measurements are used in the recipes. Some health food stores have yeast prepared without preservatives, such as Red Star brand. This yeast will provide the lightest results.

Yoghurt: plain yoghurt, made without sugar

How to Convert Your Favorite Recipe to Natural Ingredients

Most recipes are adaptable to natural ingredients. Use pastry flour in cookies, cakes and pies. Use bread flour in unyeasted and yeasted breads. Use less whole grain flour than the amount of white flour given; if the recipe calls for 1 cup white flour, use ⅔ to ¾ cup whole grain flour. Substitute less oil than the solid shortening required; if the recipe calls for ½ cup shortening, use about ⅓ cup oil. Use less honey than the amount of sugar listed. Honey is twice as sweet-tasting as sugar. If the recipe calls for 1 cup sugar, only ½ cup honey may be needed to achieve the same sweetness.

When using liquid oil and liquid sweeteners, the amount of other liquid found in the recipe will have to be reduced by approximately the same amount as the additional liquid to avoid making the batter or dough too wet. Even with these adjustments, the batter will be moister than usual. To bake thoroughly and avoid any raw middles, bake at a lower temperature for a longer time. Reduce the suggested temperature by 25° and watch it carefully to determine the proper baking time.

Dairy Foods

To lower the intake of concentrated fats, some people prefer not to use dairy products. Here are some suggested substitutes.

Milk used in baking can be substituted with soy and nut milks for very similar results. Use 1 cup soy or nut milk to 1 cup regular milk. Fruit juice or potato water can also be used as a substitute in the same amounts suggested for the milk. For fruit juice, reduce the sweetener in the recipe, as fruit juice adds sweetness.

Soy Milk (*Quick Method*)   MAKES 3 QUARTS

1 pound soy flour
3 quarts cold water
2 tablespoons honey
1 teaspoon vanilla
½ teaspoon sea salt

In the top of a double boiler, beat the flour and water with a wire whisk until smooth. Cook over rapidly boiling water for 25 minutes, stirring often. Strain the milk through a piece of fine cheesecloth. Stir in the honey, vanilla and salt. Store in a covered jar in the refrigerator. Shake before using.

Soy Milk (*Slow Method*)   MAKES 2 QUARTS

⅔ cup soybeans
4 cups water
⅓ cup oil
¼ cup honey
¼ teaspoon sea salt

Place the beans in a pot with water to cover and soak for 8 to 10 hours, or overnight.

Drain beans, reserving the soaking water, add enough water to make the soaking water 4 cups. Place the beans in a blender with 2 cups of the water and blend at medium speed for 3 minutes. Pour into the top of a double boiler, stir in the remaining water, and cook over rapidly boiling water for 30 minutes.

Strain the milk through a piece of fine cheesecloth. Pour the strained milk back into the rinsed double boiler. Cook for 30 minutes more over rapidly boiling water, and strain. Pour ⅔ cup of the milk into the blender; add the oil and blend for 5 minutes at medium speed. Add the remaining milk, honey and salt and blend for 2 minutes more. Store in a covered container in the refrigerator. Shake before using. Use within a week.

Almond Milk

1 cup almonds
1 quart cold water
2 tablespoons honey
¼ teaspoon sea salt
1 tablespoon oil

Blanch the almonds by covering them with boiling water; allow to cool. Remove the skins. Place the almonds and remaining ingredients in a blender and blend for 3 minutes at medium speed. Strain through a piece of fine cheesecloth. Store in an airtight container in the refrigerator. Shake before using. Use within a week.

Cashew Milk

1 cup cashews
4 cups cold water
1 tablespoon honey
¼ teaspoon sea salt

Place all the ingredients in a blender and blend at medium to high speed for 3 minutes. Strain through a piece of fine cheesecloth. Store in a covered jar in the refrigerator. Shake before using.

Note: All of these milks will leave a pulp when strained through cheesecloth that can be added to cookies, cakes and bread doughs for added nutrition.

Butter can be substituted with soy margarine which provides a similar flavor and texture. It is available in health food stores. It is particularly good in Scottish Shortbread or for flavor in puddings.

Corn oil also can be substituted for all or part of the butter called for in a recipe. Use 1 part butter to 2 parts oil, or use only oil, reducing the amount of liquid indicated in the recipe.

Eggs can be left out of many of the recipes. Simply increase the amount of liquid by approximately ¼ cup per egg to compensate.

Sour Cream is called for in some of the recipes. Here is a substitute.

Tofu Sour Cream

MAKES 1 CUP

8 ounces tofu (soybean curd)
Juice of 1 lemon
½ teaspoon sea salt

Place the tofu into boiling, salted water to cover. Remove from heat and allow to stand for 2 to 3 minutes. Place the tofu in a piece of fine cheesecloth and squeeze to expel the excess liquid. Place the tofu, lemon juice and salt in a blender and blend at medium to high speed until smooth. If too sour, add more salt.

Suggested Utensils

For Food Preparation

Blender: for preparing nut milks or bread crumbs

Bowls: small, medium and large sizes

Bread board: 2′ x 1½′ is adequate for kneading dough and rolling out crusts

Cutters: small and large cookie cutters in various shapes

Egg beater: hand operated

Fork: with long tines

Grater: adequate size for grating cheese

Knife: small sizes to peel fruits and one with a larger blade for handling cookies

Measuring cups: 1 cup, ½ cup, ⅓ cup and ¼ cup measures

Measuring spoons: 1 tablespoon, 1 teaspoon, ½ teaspoon, and ¼ teaspoon sizes

Mixer: electric for whipping egg white or cream

Pastry brush: for brushing surfaces with egg whites

Potato masher: for mashing bananas for Banana Bread

Rolling pin: for cookies, pie and bread doughs

Scissors: for cutting dried fruits

Sifter: double-screen sifter is good for whole grain flour

Spatula: rubber and metal, for scraping and turning

Wire whisk: for beating

Wooden spoons: several sizes. Will help prevent scratches on pans

For Cooking and Baking

Baking dish: for puddings, 1½- to 2-quart sizes

Baking sheets: 14" x 10" or 17" x 14", without sides

Cake pans: 8" round; 13" x 9" oblong or rectangular; 8" or 9" square

Loaf pans: 7⅞" x 3⅞" or 8½" x 4½"

Muffin tins: 2 with small or medium cups

Pie plates: 9" round

Saucepans: 1- and 2-quart sizes

Springform pan: for cheesecake, 9" round

Waffle iron

Wire racks: for cooling

Try to avoid using any pans that might leave a residue on the food, such as aluminum and teflon pans. Replace these pans with ones of better quality, such as stainless steel or black baker's steel. For glass baking dishes, reduce the suggested oven temperature by 25°.

Glossary of Terms

Bake: cook by dry heat in an oven

Beat: mix by stirring vigorously until the batter is smooth

Blanch: plunge into boiling water, drain, then allow to cool and remove skins (nuts and fruits)

Blend: mix thoroughly, sometimes using an electric blender

Boil: cook liquid over direct heat until bubbles break the surface

Chill: cool thoroughly in the refrigerator

Chop: cut into fine or coarse pieces with a sharp knife

Cream: beat fat and sweetener to a creamy consistency by forcing the mixture against the sides of the bowl with a wooden spoon

Cut in: combine fat and flour by cutting through the mixture repeatedly with a fork or pastry blender

Drain: remove liquid by placing ingredient in strainer or colander and allowing liquid to run off, discarding it or reserving it for later use

Drop: form cookies by pushing batter off of the spoon to "drop" onto a baking sheet

Fold: blend ingredients by cutting through the middle with a spoon or rubber spatula and bring the batter up near the edge of the bowl and fold over. Turn the bowl as you fold to thoroughly combine the ingredients.

Grate: rub food against a grater to shred

Knead: work flour into dough by pressing and folding

Mash: crush in a bowl with a masher until a soft, uniform consistency

Mix: combine ingredients by stirring with a spoon

Oil: rub a thin layer of lubricant on baking pans to prevent sticking

Roast: cook by dry heat in an oven until crisp

Roll out: spread dough out on a board to a desired thickness using a rolling pin

Scald: cook milk over medium heat until bubbles form around the edge or a skin forms over the top (approximately 180°F.)

Separate eggs: separate the white from the egg yolk. Crack the egg in half over a bowl, allowing the yolk to fall into half of the shell and the white to run over the edge of the shell into the bowl. Transfer the yolk back and forth between the shell halves until all of the white is in the bowl without any yolk. Place the yolk in a separate bowl.

Sift: to pass through a sifter or screen to remove lumps and incorporate air

Simmer: cook liquid at just below an active boil. Steam should rise from the surface, but no bubbles should break the surface.

Steam: cook in the steam from actively boiling liquid

Stir: mix in a circular motion with a wooden spoon

Toast: cook over direct heat until brown

Whip: beat at high speed with an electric mixer, to incorporate air, until stiff

Equivalents

All of the measurements used in baking, including the measuring cups and spoons used for dry measure, are liquid measurement amounts.

1 teaspoon	=	⅓ tablespoon
1 tablespoon	=	3 teaspoons
¼ cup	=	4 tablespoons
⅓ cup	=	5⅓ tablespoons
½ cup	=	8 tablespoons
1 cup	=	16 tablespoons
2 cups	=	1 pint
2 pints	=	1 quart
4 quarts	=	1 gallon

Metric Conversion Chart

¼ teaspoon	=	1.25 millilitres
½ teaspoon	=	2.5 millilitres
1 teaspoon	=	5 millilitres
1 tablespoon	=	15 millilitres
¼ cup	=	63 millilitres
⅓ cup	=	84 millilitres
½ cup	=	125 millilitres
1 cup	=	¼ litre or 250 millilitres
1 pint	=	.473 litre
1 quart	=	.946 litre
1 ounce	=	30 grams
1 pound	=	454 grams

Cookies

How To Make Cookies

Drop Cookies are made by dropping the batter onto the cookie sheet by the rounded teaspoonful. The batter should be stiff enough to hold its shape when dropped. Any differences in the handling of the batter are listed in the individual recipes.

To Prepare the Batter:

1: Read the whole recipe. Preheat the oven.
2: Set out the ingredients and put each one away as it is added to the batter to insure that all the ingredients are added.
3: Measure the oil in a liquid measuring cup. Coat the sides of the cup with the oil and pour it into a medium-sized bowl.
4: Measure the sweetener in the oily measuring cup. Add to the oil; it will slip easily out of the cup.
5: Beat the egg in the same measuring cup. Pour into the bowl and stir until blended evenly.
   Optional Eggs: Some people prefer not to use eggs. The egg can be left out of most of these recipes by adding ¼ cup more liquid or reducing the amount of flour listed. In Coconut Puffs and Carob Brownies, the egg is used as leavening and must be kept in.
6: Add the dry ingredients. Add the flour in small amounts until the desired stiffness is reached. Pastry flour is called for in most of the recipes, but whole wheat bread flour may be substituted. If used, reduce the amount of flour or add more liquid as the bread flour is more absorbent. These cookies will be slightly heavier.
7: Lightly oil a baking sheet, or cake pan turned upside down. Drop the cookies onto the sheet, leaving 2" between cookies to allow for spreading during baking.
8: Cookies made with liquid sweeteners tend to be raw in the middle if not of uniform thickness. For this reason, be sure to follow the individual recipes in regard to shaping and baking the cookies.
9: Cookies are ready when the center feels firm when touched lightly. Times and temperatures required for baking can vary from oven to oven, so watch the first few batches to prevent burning.

Bar Cookies are baked in an oiled 9″ x 9″ cake pan and cut into squares or bars after baking. The batter is thicker than a cake batter, but not stiff. It should be spread evenly and into the corners of the pan. The cookies are done when they pull away from the sides of the pan and the middle feels firm.

Holiday Cookies often take extra effort to prepare and are usually made on special occasions, but these delicious recipes are worth preparing for any occasion. Gingerbread Men, Date-Filled and Scottish Shortbread are rolled cookies. The batter is a soft dough that is rolled out to a specific thickness and cut into shapes with floured cookie cutters. One easy way to transfer the cookies from the cutting board to the baking sheet is to slip a wide-bladed knife under the cookie and lift it onto the sheet. These cookies are done baking when firm to the touch. Peanut Butter Balls are uncooked cookies.

"Natural foods" means no preservatives, so cool the cookies completely before storing in airtight containers. Any condensation from warm cookies will hasten the growth of mold. Refrigerate the cookies if storing them for more than 2 or 3 days. Most of the cookies can be frozen for later use, but should be eaten within a few days of thawing as frozen foods lose their freshness quickly. It is best to store them in the refrigerator after thawing.

Granola Cookies

½ cup oil
⅓ cup honey
3 tablespoons molasses
2 cups Maple-Walnut Granola (see recipe)
1 teaspoon sea salt
1 teaspoon baking powder
¼ cup wheat germ
⅔ cup rye flour

1: Oil a baking sheet and preheat oven to 350°F.
2: In a medium-sized mixing bowl, combine the oil, honey and molasses.
3: Stir in the granola.
4: Add the salt, baking powder and wheat germ, stirring well.
5: Fold in the flour to form a batter that is crumbly and feels oily.
6: Drop the batter onto the baking sheet by the rounded teaspoonful. Place 3″ apart to allow for spreading during baking. Shape the drops of batter into round cookies of uniform thickness.
7: Bake for 10 minutes; the middle of the cookie should be firm and the edges browned when done.
8: Allow the cookies to cool before removing from the baking sheet. Bake all of the cookies and cool thoroughly on wire racks. Store in an airtight container.

Vanilla Cookies

⅓ cup oil
⅔ cup honey or maple syrup
1 teaspoon vanilla
1 egg
1¾ cups pastry flour

1: Oil a baking sheet and preheat oven to 375°F.
2: In a medium-sized mixing bowl, combine the oil, honey and vanilla.
3: Beat the egg and stir into the oil mixture.
4: Gradually stir in enough of the flour to form a stiff batter.
5: Drop the batter onto an oiled baking sheet by the rounded teaspoonful.
6: Bake for 10 minutes.
7: Bake all of the cookies and cool thoroughly on wire racks. Store in an airtight container.

VARIATIONS:

Toll House Cookies: Fold ⅓ cup carob chips and ½ cup chopped walnuts into the finished batter before baking.

Raisin Cookies: Fold ½ cup raisins into the finished batter before baking. Or, fold ½ cup any chopped dried fruit or nuts into the finished batter before baking.

Carob Cookies

¼ cup oil
⅔ cup honey
1 teaspoon vanilla
1 egg
½ cup carob powder
½ teaspoon sea salt
½ teaspoon baking soda
1 cup pastry flour
½ cup chopped walnuts

1: Oil a baking sheet and preheat oven to 375°F.
2: In a medium-sized bowl, combine the oil, honey and vanilla.
3: Beat the egg and stir into the oil mixture.
4: Sift together the carob, salt and baking soda and stir into the liquid ingredients.
5: Gradually add the flour to make a firm batter.
6: Fold in the nuts.
7: Drop the batter onto the baking sheet by the rounded teaspoonful.
8: Bake for 10 minutes.
9: Bake all of the cookies and cool on wire racks. Store in an airtight container.

VARIATIONS:
Add ½ cup chopped pecans, coconut, or carob chips to the finished batter before baking.

Oatmeal Cookies

1 cup raisins
1 cup water
⅓ cup oil
⅔ cup honey
1 teaspoon vanilla
1 egg
2 cups rolled oats
½ teaspoon baking powder
1 teaspoon baking soda
1 teaspoon sea salt
1 teaspoon cinnamon
½ teaspoon cloves
1 cup pastry flour
½ cup chopped walnuts

1: In a small saucepan, combine the raisins and the water and simmer over low heat until raisins are plump.
2: Remove from heat and drain the remaining liquid into a measuring cup; add enough water to make ½ cup liquid and set aside.
3: Oil a baking sheet and preheat oven to 375°F.
4: In a medium-sized mixing bowl, combine the oil, honey and vanilla.
5: Beat the egg and stir into the oil mixture.
6: Stir in the raisin liquid.
7: Add the rolled oats and mix well.
8: Stir in the remaining ingredients, except for the flour, walnuts and raisins.
9: Gradually blend in enough of the flour to make a firm batter.
10: Fold in the raisins and nuts.
11: Drop the batter onto the baking sheet by the rounded teaspoonful.
12: Bake for 10 minutes.
13: Bake all of the cookies and cool on a wire rack. Store in an airtight container.

Peanut Butter Cookies

MAKES 3 DOZEN

¼ cup oil
½ cup honey
1 cup chunky peanut butter
1 egg
1½ cups pastry flour
½ cup chopped, roasted peanuts (see below)

1: Oil a baking sheet and preheat oven to 350°F.
2: In a medium-sized bowl combine the oil, honey and peanut butter.
3: Beat the egg and stir into the oil mixture.
4: Gradually add enough of the flour to make a stiff batter.
5: Fold in the peanuts.
6: Drop the batter onto the baking sheet by the rounded teaspoonful.
7: Using the tines of a fork, press the cookies down to an even thickness.
8: Bake for 15 minutes.
9: Bake all of the cookies and cool thoroughly on a wire rack. Store in an airtight container.

Roasted Peanuts: Place the raw peanuts in a shallow pan; roast in a 300°F. oven for 20 minutes, stirring frequently. Cool a few of the nuts and taste to test for crunchiness.

VARIATION:
Peanut Butter Sandwiches: Sweeten ½ cup of peanut butter with 2 tablespoons of molasses. Spread approximately ½ teaspoon of this mixture on a cookie and cover with another cookie.

Coconut Puffs

3 egg whites
½ teaspoon vanilla
2 tablespoons honey
1 cup toasted coconut (see below)
¼ cup finely chopped walnuts

1: Oil a baking sheet and preheat oven to 350°F.
2: Using an electric mixer, whip the egg whites in a medium-sized bowl until stiff.
3: Add the vanilla and honey, and continue beating with the electric mixer until well blended.
4: Fold in the coconut and the walnuts.
5: Drop the batter onto the baking sheet by the rounded teaspoonful.
6: Bake for 10 minutes.
7: Allow the cookies to cool before removing from the baking sheet.
8: Bake all of the cookies and cool thoroughly on wire racks. Store in an airtight container.

Toasted Coconut: Spread the coconut in a shallow pan; toast in a 325°F. oven for approximately 10 minutes, stirring frequently until golden-brown. Cool before using.

Leftover egg yolks? Try Vanilla Pudding or Carob Pudding.

Hermits

⅓ cup oil
½ cup honey
½ cup sour cream
1 egg
¾ teaspoon cinnamon
½ teaspoon cloves
¼ teaspoon baking soda
1½ to 2 cups pastry flour
½ cup raisins
½ cup chopped walnuts

1: Oil a baking sheet and preheat oven to 375°F.
2: In a medium-sized bowl, combine the oil, honey and sour cream.
3: Beat the egg and stir into the oil mixture.
4: Stir in the spices and baking soda.
5: Gradually add enough of the flour to form a firm batter.
6: Fold in the raisins and nuts.
7: Drop the batter onto the baking sheet by the rounded tea-spoonful.
8: Bake for 15 minutes.
9: Bake all of the cookies and cool on a wire rack. Store in an air-tight container.

Carob Brownies

2 eggs
⅓ cup oil
½ cup honey
½ teaspoon vanilla
6 tablespoons carob powder
½ teaspoon sea salt
½ cup pastry flour
1 cup chopped walnuts

1: Oil a 9″ x 9″ pan and preheat oven to 350°F.
2: Separate the eggs. In a medium-sized bowl, combine the egg yolks, oil, honey and vanilla.
3: Sift together the carob and salt; stir into the oil mixture.
4: Stir in the flour until evenly blended. The batter should be stiff and dry.
5: Mix in the nuts.
6: Using an electric mixer, whip the egg whites in a medium-sized bowl until stiff.
7: Gently fold the egg whites into the carob mixture.
8: Spread the batter evenly in the pan.
9: Bake for 30 minutes.
10: Cut the brownies into squares while hot. Cool in the pan on a wire rack. Store in an airtight container.

Wheat Germ Brownies

¼ cup oil
¼ cup molasses
½ cup honey
1 teaspoon vanilla
1 egg
¼ teaspoon sea salt
½ teaspoon baking powder
1 cup wheat germ
½ cup pastry flour
½ cup chopped nuts

1: Oil a 9″ x 9″ pan and preheat oven to 350°F.
2. In a medium-sized bowl, combine the oil, molasses, honey and vanilla.
3: Beat the egg and stir into the oil mixture.
4: Stir in the salt, baking powder and wheat germ, until evenly blended.
5: Stir in the flour.
6: Fold in the nuts.
7: Spread the batter evenly in the pan.
8: Bake for 30 minutes.
9: Cut into squares while hot. Cool in the pan on a wire rack. Store in an airtight container.

Fig Bars

Filling:
1½ cups chopped figs
⅔ cup water
¼ cup honey
1 teaspoon grated lemon rind
½ cup finely chopped walnuts
½ cup shredded coconut

1: Place the figs, water and honey in a small saucepan and simmer over low heat until the mixture cooks down to a paste.
2: Remove mixture from the heat; stir in the lemon rind, walnuts and coconut and set aside.

Crust:
⅓ cup oil
⅓ cup honey
½ teaspoon vanilla
½ teaspoon sea salt
1½ cups pastry flour
1½ cups rolled oats

1: Oil a 9″ x 9″ pan and preheat oven to 350°F.
2: In a medium-sized bowl, combine the oil, honey and vanilla.
3: Stir in the salt and flour.
4: Add enough rolled oats to form a crumbly mixture.
5: Spread half of the crust mixture into the pan.
6: Cover crust mixture with the filling.
7: Spread the other half of the crust mixture on top of the filling.
8: Bake for 30 minutes.
9: While still hot, cut into small bars and allow to cool in the pan, on a wire rack. Store bars in an airtight container.

Gingerbread Men

¼ cup oil
¼ cup honey
½ cup molasses
½ cup water
½ teaspoon sea salt
1 teaspoon baking soda
¼ teaspoon cloves
½ teaspoon cinnamon
1¼ teaspoons ginger
3½ to 4 cups sifted pastry flour
Approximately ¼ cup raisins or currants

1: In a medium-sized bowl, combine the oil, honey, molasses and water.
2: Stir in the salt, baking soda, and spices.
3: Add 1 cup of the flour to the liquid mixture, blending well.
4: Gradually stir in the remaining flour, ½ cup at a time, to avoid making the dough too dry. When the dough forms a mass that pulls away from the sides of the bowl, stop adding flour. The surface of the dough should feel sticky and soft.
5: Cover the bowl and chill the dough in the refrigerator for 3 to 4 hours or overnight.
6: Oil a baking sheet and preheat oven to 350°F.
7: On a lightly floured board, roll out one-half of the dough ¼″ to ⅜″ thick.
8: Cut the dough into gingerbread men (or other desired shapes) with cookie cutters that have been dipped in flour to prevent sticking.
9: Using a wide-bladed knife, transfer the gingerbread shapes to the baking sheet.
10: Form the remaining scraps of dough into a smooth ball. Roll out and cut more cookies.
11: Repeat the process with the remaining dough.
12: Make the eyes and buttons for the gingerbread men with raisins or currants.
13: Bake for 10 to 15 minutes. Bake all of the cookies and cool on wire racks. Store in an airtight container.

Date-Filled Cookies

Dough:
½ cup soft butter
⅓ cup maple syrup or honey
½ teaspoon sea salt
1 teaspoon baking powder
1 teaspoon vanilla
1 egg, beaten
2 cups pastry flour

1: In a medium-sized mixing bowl, cream together the butter and maple syrup until smooth.
2: Add the salt, baking powder and vanilla and stir well.
3: Beat the egg and stir into the butter mixture.
4: Gradually add enough of the flour to form one solid mass of dough that pulls away from the sides of the bowl. Don't make the dough too dry; more flour will be added when the dough is rolled out.
5: Cover the bowl and place in the refrigerator. Chill for several hours or overnight.
6: Prepare the filling before removing the dough from the refrigerator to roll out.

Filling:
2 cups chopped dates
⅔ cup water
¼ cup maple syrup or honey
½ cup finely chopped walnuts
1 tablespoon lemon juice

1: Using wet scissors or a knife, cut the dates into small pieces.
2: In a small saucepan, combine the dates, water and maple syrup. Cook over medium-low heat until it forms a thick paste.
3: Remove from heat and stir in the nuts and lemon juice.
4: Set aside while you roll out the dough and cut the cookies.

To Form the Cookies:
1: Oil 2 or more baking sheets and preheat the oven to 350°F.
2: On a lightly-floured board, roll out the dough to ¼" thick.
3: Using a round cookie cutter or the rim of a glass, dipped in flour

to prevent sticking, cut the dough into circles approximately 3″ in diameter. Reserve the scraps of dough to rework and make more cookies.

4: Place approximately ½ teaspoon of date filling in the middle of each circle of dough.

5: Fold the dough in half over the filling.

6: Using a fork that has been dipped in flour to prevent sticking, press the dough together around the open edge of the cookie, sealing in the filling.

7: Lift the cookies from the board onto the baking sheet. Bake for 20 minutes.

8: Remove the cookies from the sheets and cool thoroughly on wire racks. Store in an airtight container.

Peanut Butter Balls

MAKES 3 DOZEN

½ cup chopped dates
½ cup chopped raisins
1 cup coarsely chopped walnuts
¼ cup molasses
1 cup chunky peanut butter
1 to 2 tablespoons orange juice (unsweetened)
½ cup shredded coconut

1: Using a wet knife or scissors cut the dates and raisins into small pieces. Combine the walnuts, dates and raisins in a medium-sized bowl.

2: Stir in the molasses.

3: Add the peanut butter, stirring until the fruit and nuts are evenly distributed.

4: Stir in enough orange juice to moisten the mixture.

5: Roll a teaspoonful of batter into a small ball, then roll the ball in the coconut. Form all of the batter into balls.

6: Store in an airtight container. The flavor of these cookies is enhanced after a day of storage.

Scottish Shortbread

The flavor of shortbread improves after a day or two in the refrigerator, so make it in advance for the holidays.

> ¼ pound butter or soy margarine
> ¼ cup honey or maple syrup
> 1½ to 2 cups pastry flour

1: Preheat oven to 350°F.
2: In a medium-sized bowl, cream together the butter and sweetener.
3: Sift the flour and add to the butter mixture in ½ cup amounts until the dough forms a ball. Avoid making too dry a dough, since more flour will be added during the rolling out and handling.
4: On a lightly floured board, roll out the dough ⅜" to ½" thick.
5: Cut dough into small shapes with floured cookie cutters. (Shortbread is very rich so smaller cookies are best.)
6: Using a wide-bladed knife, transfer the cookies to an ungreased baking sheet.
7: Bake for 15 to 20 minutes. Some browning will occur, but cookies will not change shape.
8: Cool on wire racks, and store in an airtight container.

VARIATION:

Maple-Coconut Bars: Prepare the shortbread dough and, using a rubber spatula, press it into a buttered 9" square pan. Combine 1 cup coconut, ½ cup maple syrup, and ¼ teaspoon sea salt in a small saucepan. Place over low heat and cook, stirring frequently, until the syrup is absorbed. Spread evenly over the shortbread dough. Bake at 350°F. for 30 minutes until topping is golden brown. While still hot, cut shortbread into bars. Then place pan of shortbread on a wire rack and allow to cool. Remove bars and store in an airtight container. Makes 16 squares.

Cakes

How to Make a Cake

Cakes made with whole wheat flour have a heavier texture than those made with white flour.

To Prepare the Batter:
1: Read the whole recipe. Preheat the oven.
2: Set out the ingredients and put each one away as it is added to the batter.
3: Sift together the dry ingredients onto a sheet of waxed paper. When whole grain flour is sifted, a coarse chaff remains; save this and add it to bread dough. Or, for added nutrition leave the chaff in the cake by blending, rather than sifting, the dry ingredients together before adding to the batter. Pastry flour is called for in the cake recipes in order to obtain the lightest results. However, whole wheat bread flour can be used if the amount of flour is decreased or the amount of liquid is increased to attain the desired batter texture.
4: Measure the oil in a liquid measuring cup. Coat the sides of the cup with the oil, and pour into a medium or large bowl.
5: Measure the liquid sweetener in the oily measuring cup. Add to the bowl with the oil; it will slip easily out of the cup.
6: Beat the egg in the same measuring cup; add to the oil mixture, stirring until evenly blended.
   Optional Eggs: Eggs can be left out of most of these recipes; simply add ¼ cup more liquid to the recipe or use less flour. In the Maple-Walnut Cake and Cheesecake, eggs are used for leavening and must be left in.
7: Add ⅓ of the dry ingredients to the mixture in the bowl, stirring in until evenly blended.
8: Stir in ⅓ of the milk or water listed in the recipe, blending until smooth.
9: Add the remaining ⅔ of the dry ingredients, ⅓ at a time, alternately with the remaining liquid, stirring well after each addition. The finished batter should be liquid enough to pour from the bowl.
10: Pour the batter into a lightly oiled baking pan, spreading evenly to the edges of the pan.

11: Place the cake in the oven and bake. The cake is done when it pulls away from the sides of the pan or the center springs back when lightly touched.
12: Cool the cake in the pan on a wire rack. If desired, add a topping before serving.

Spice Cake

½ cup raisins
½ cup water
3 cups pastry flour
1 teaspoon sea salt
3 teaspoons baking powder
½ teaspoon cinnamon
¼ teaspoon each cloves, allspice and nutmeg
⅓ cup oil
1 cup honey
1 teaspoon vanilla
2 eggs
¾ cup milk

1: Oil a 9″ x 13″ baking pan and preheat oven to 350°F.
2: Combine the raisins and water in a small saucepan and simmer over low heat until soft and plump.
3: Drain off the excess water and set the raisins aside.
4: Sift together the dry ingredients and set aside.
5: In a large bowl mix together the oil, honey and vanilla.
6: Beat the eggs and add to the oil mixture, stirring well.
7: Add the dry ingredients alternately with the milk, stirring well after each addition.
8: Fold in the raisins.
9: Pour the batter into the pan.
10: Sprinkle the surface of the cake with topping (recipe below).
11: Bake for 40 minutes.
12: Cool the cake in the pan on a wire rack.

Spice Cake Topping

2 tablespoons soft butter
¼ cup honey
½ cup coconut
¼ cup chopped walnuts

1: In a small bowl, blend all the ingredients together to form a crumbly mixture.

Carob Cake

2¼ cups pastry flour
⅔ cup powdered carob
¼ teaspoon baking powder
1¼ teaspoons baking soda
1 teaspoon sea salt
½ cup oil
⅔ cup honey
1 teaspoon vanilla
2 eggs
¾ cup water

1: Oil a 9″ x 13″ baking pan and preheat oven to 350°F.
2: Sift together the dry ingredients and set aside.
3: In a large bowl, combine the oil, honey and vanilla.
4: Beat the eggs and add to the oil mixture, stirring well.
5: Add the dry ingredients alternately with the water, stirring well after each addition.
6: Pour the batter into the baking pan.
7: Bake for 40 minutes.
8: Cool the cake in the pan on a wire rack.

VARIATIONS:
Fold approximately ½ cup chopped walnuts, pecans, coconut or carob chips into the finished batter before baking.

Sprinkle the batter with the Spice Cake Topping (see recipe) before baking.

Vanilla Cake

2 cups pastry flour
½ teaspoon sea salt
1 teaspoon baking soda
¼ cup oil
½ cup honey
1 teaspoon vanilla
1 egg
½ cup milk

1: Oil a 9″ x 9″ baking pan and preheat oven to 350°F.
2: Sift together the dry ingredients and set aside.
3: In a medium-sized bowl, combine the oil, honey and vanilla.
4: Beat the egg and stir into the oil mixture.
5: Add the dry ingredients alternately with the milk, stirring well after each addition.
6: Pour the batter into the baking pan.
7: Bake for 35 minutes.
8: Cool the cake in the pan on a wire rack.

VARIATION:
Fold ⅓ cup coconut, nuts, raisins or berries into the batter before baking, or top with a Cheesecake Fruit Topping (see recipe) before serving.

Applesauce Cake

2 cups pastry flour
½ teaspoon sea salt
1 teaspoon baking soda
½ teaspoon cinnamon
¼ teaspoon each cloves and allspice
¼ cup oil
½ cup honey
1 cup applesauce
1 egg
½ cup raisins
½ cup chopped walnuts

1: Oil a 9" x 9" baking pan and preheat oven to 350°F.
2: Sift together the dry ingredients and set aside.
3: In a medium-sized bowl, combine the oil, honey and applesauce.
4: Beat the egg and stir into the oil mixture.
5: Gradually stir in the dry ingredients.
6: Fold in the raisins and nuts.
7: Pour the batter into the pan.
8: Bake for 40 minutes.
9: Cool cake in the pan on a wire rack.

Gingerbread

2¼ cups pastry flour
½ teaspoon sea salt
1 teaspoon baking soda
1¼ teaspoons ginger
1 teaspoon cinnamon
½ cup oil
2 tablespoons honey
1 cup molasses
1 egg
⅔ cup boiling water

1: Oil a 9" x 9" baking pan and preheat oven to 325°F.
2: Sift together the dry ingredients and set aside.
3: In a medium-sized bowl, combine the oil, honey and molasses.
4: Beat the egg and stir into the oil mixture.
5: Mix in the boiling water.
6: Gradually stir in the dry ingredients.
7: Pour the batter into the baking pan.
8: Bake for 45 minutes.
9: Cool cake in the pan on a wire rack. Serve plain or topped with Sweetened Whipped Cream or Applesauce (see recipe).

Maple-Walnut Cake

3 cups pastry flour
3 teaspoons baking powder
1 teaspoon sea salt
2 eggs, separated
⅓ cup oil
⅔ cup maple syrup
1½ teaspoons vanilla
1 cup milk
½ cup finely chopped walnuts

1: Oil and flour two 8" round cake pans or a 9" x 13" baking pan and preheat oven to 375°F.
2: Sift together the dry ingredients and set aside.
3: In a large bowl, combine the egg yolks, oil, syrup and vanilla.
4: Add the dry ingredients alternately with the milk, stirring well after each addition.
5: Stir in the walnuts.
6: Using an electric mixer, in a medium-sized bowl, whip the egg whites until stiff.
7: Gently fold the egg whites into the batter.
8: Pour the batter into the cake pans.
9: Bake for 35 minutes if in two cake pans, for 40 minutes if in one rectangular pan.
10: Remove the layers from the pans and cool on a wire rack. The rectangular cake should be cooled in the pan on a wire rack.
11: Slice each layer in half crosswise to form 4 layers.
12: Fill and frost the layers with Pineapple Cream Icing (recipe below). For the single rectangular cake make only half of the icing recipe.
13: Chill the frosted cake for at least 2 hours before serving.
14: Cut into wedges with a hot, sharp knife. (Hold the knife under hot water to heat, and dry before using.)

Pineapple Cream Icing

12 ounces soft cream cheese, at room temperature
Pineapple juice (reserved from crushed pineapple)
1 cup whipping cream
2 tablespoons honey
½ teaspoon vanilla
¼ cup crushed unsweetened pineapple, drained

1: In a medium-sized bowl, combine 1 to 2 tablespoons of the pineapple juice and all the cream cheese. Using an electric mixer, beat until smooth, but still thick.
2: In a separate bowl, using an electric mixer, whip the cream until stiff.
3: Using the mixer, beat the honey and vanilla into the whipped cream.
4: Add the whipped cream to the cream cheese and beat with the electric mixer until smooth.
5: Fold in the crushed pineapple.
6: Chill the icing for approximately 2 hours until firm.
7: Spread half the icing between the cake layers.
8: Spread the remaining half of the icing over the top and sides of the cake.
9: Chill frosted cake before serving.

Cheesecake

Crust:
½ cup Graham cracker crumbs
1 tablespoon date sugar
¼ teaspoon cinnamon
¼ teaspoon nutmeg

1: In a small bowl, blend all the ingredients together.
2: Butter the sides and bottom of a 9'' springform pan.
3: Press the crumb mixture into the bottom and sides of the pan.

Filling:
5 eggs, separated
⅔ cup honey
1 pound cream cheese, at room temperature
1 cup sour cream
1 teaspoon vanilla
½ cup pastry flour

1: Preheat oven to 300°F.
2: In a large bowl, using an electric mixer, beat the egg yolks until thick and lemon-colored.
3: Using the electric mixer, beat in the honey.
4: Gradually add the cream cheese, beating with the electric mixer after each addition, until smooth.
5: Beat in the sour cream and vanilla.
6: Stir in the flour.
7: Using an electric mixer, in a medium-sized bowl, whip the egg whites until stiff.
8: Fold the egg whites into the cream cheese mixture.
9: Pour the batter into the crust.
10: Bake for 1 hour.
11: Cool cake in the pan on a wire rack. Serve plain or with Fruit Topping (see recipe).

Fruit Topping for Cheesecake

1 cup fruit juice or water
2 tablespoons arrowroot
¼ cup honey
2 cups fruit or berries (fresh or frozen)

1: In a small saucepan, combine the juice, arrowroot and honey.
2: Cook over medium heat, stirring constantly, until the mixture thickens and boils.
3: Boil for 1 minute.
4: Remove from heat and fold in the fruit.
5: Cool to room temperature.
6: Serve over individual pieces of cheesecake or pour over the cooled cake and chill. Cut the cheesecake with a hot, sharp knife and serve.

Vanilla Cupcakes

3 cups pastry flour
3 teaspoons baking powder
1 teaspoon sea salt
⅓ cup oil
⅔ cup honey
1 teaspoon vanilla
2 eggs
¾ cup milk

1: Oil 2 muffin tins or line with paper or foil cups and preheat oven to 400°F.
2: Sift together the dry ingredients and set aside.
3: In a large bowl, combine the oil, honey and vanilla.
4: Beat the eggs and add to the oil mixture, stirring well.
5: Add the dry ingredients alternately with the milk, stirring well after each addition.
6: Spoon the batter into the muffin tin, filling each cup two-thirds full. Pour water into any empty cups to keep the muffin tin from losing shape in the oven.
7: Bake for 18 to 20 minutes.
8: Remove the cupcakes from the muffin tin and cool on a wire rack.

VARIATIONS:
Fold 1 cup of blueberries into the batter before pouring it into the cups.

Fold ½ cup of coconut, nuts, raisins, or berries into the batter before pouring it into the cups.

Carob Cupcakes

2½ cups pastry flour
⅔ cup carob powder
¼ teaspoon baking powder
1¼ teaspoons baking soda
1 teaspoon sea salt
½ cup oil
⅔ cup honey
1 teaspoon vanilla
2 eggs
½ cup water

1: Oil a muffin tin or line with paper or foil cups and preheat oven to 400°F.
2: Sift together the dry ingredients and set aside.
3: In a large bowl, combine the oil, honey and vanilla.
4: Beat the eggs, and add to the oil mixture, stirring well.
5: Add the dry ingredients alternately with the water, stirring well after each addition.
6: Spoon the batter into the muffin tin, filling each cup two-thirds full.
7: Bake for 18 to 20 minutes.
8: Remove cupcakes from the muffin tin and cool on a wire rack.

VARIATIONS:
Fold ½ cup walnuts, pecans, coconut or carob chips into the batter before baking.

Pies

How to Make a Pie

A whole wheat pie crust can be tricky to handle at first. While whole wheat pastry flour is called for in the pie crust recipes, you may use whole wheat bread flour at first. This makes a heavier crust, but it is easier to handle than the more fragile pastry flour crust that is also lighter and crisper. After you become familiar with the method of preparation, you can choose the flour you prefer.

To Prepare the Crust:
1: Read the whole recipe. Preheat the oven.
2: Set out the ingredients and put each one away as it is added.
3: Sift the flour into a medium-sized bowl. Stir in the salt.
4: Measure the oil in a liquid measuring cup.
5: Using a fork, stir the flour briskly while pouring in the oil in a slow, thin stream until evenly moistened.
6: Add the water in the same way as the oil. The amount of water will vary depending on the humidity, the type of oil, or the way the flour was ground. Add water until the flour mixture is moistened; there should be no dry spots in the mixture as this causes cracking when the dough is rolled out.
7: Using both hands, knead the water into the dough 3 or 4 times until the outside is slippery. If the dough is sticky, pour a little oil onto the dough and work it in so that the crust will not stick to the waxed paper when rolled out.

For a Double-Crust Pie:
8: Form ½ of the dough into a smooth ball. Place in the center of an 18"-long sheet of waxed paper. Pat down the dough until it is round and of even thickness.
9: Cover the dough with another 18"-long sheet of waxed paper. Using a rolling pin, roll out the dough to about ¼" thick to make a circle of crust with the diameter equal to the width of the paper. This crust will fit a 9" pie plate.
10: Carefully peel off the top sheet of waxed paper, lift the crust, along with the bottom sheet of waxed paper, and flip it over into a pie plate. Gently lower the crust as far as possible into the plate while still on the paper, handling it as little as possible once the remaining sheet of paper is removed.

11: Remove the second sheet of paper, slowly peeling it away from the crust and using a knife to gently separate the crust from the paper in any spots that stick.

12: Spread your fingers out along the edge of the crust to hold it and pull it away from the sides while lowering it into the plate. Do not push it down and break the crust. If the crust does break, repair by patting in a patch of dough and smoothing the edges down.

If the crust falls apart, it is probably too dry. Roll the crust into a ball, add a little more water and roll the dough out again. This dough can be kneaded several times, so keep trying. If it is impossible to place the crust in the pie plate in one piece, press the dough evenly into the sides and bottom of the plate. The top crust does not require as much handling and can usually be rolled out and placed on top of the pie with no problem.

13: Fill the crust with the filling indicated in the recipe.

14: Roll out the second half of the dough, using the same method as for the bottom crust.

15: Remove the top sheet of waxed paper from the crust. Lift the bottom sheet of waxed paper with the crust and flip it over on top of the filled pie.

16: Gently peel off the waxed paper.

17: Finish the edges of the pie by pressing them together with the tines of a fork dipped in flour to prevent sticking.

18: Trim the ragged edge of the crust by cutting around the edge of the pie plate with a sharp knife. If there is leftover crust try Roll-ups (see recipe).

19: Using a pointed knife, cut 4 or 5 short slashes in the center of the top crust to allow for the release of steam during baking.

20: Bake according to the recipe.

For a Single-Crust Pie

Use half the amount of each ingredient and follow the same procedure as for a double-crust pie, steps 1 through 12. Then follow these steps:

13: Press the dough up along the edge of the plate to form an even ridge.

14: Using the index finger and thumb, pinch the ridge of dough into ripples; bring the outer edge of the ripple over the edge of the pie plate to prevent the crust from shrinking during baking.

15: Bake according to the recipe.

Whole Wheat Pie Crust: Double-Crust Pie

2 cups whole wheat pastry flour
½ teaspoon sea salt
½ cup oil
½ cup cold water

1: In a medium-sized bowl, sift together the flour and salt.
2: Stir in the oil.
3: Stir in the water and knead the dough 3 or 4 times until moist.
4: Divide the dough into 2 portions; roll out one portion.
5: Place the bottom crust in the pie plate.
6: Roll out the remaining dough for the top crust.

Whole Wheat Pie Crust: Single-Crust Pie

1 cup whole wheat pastry flour
¼ teaspoon sea salt
¼ cup oil
¼ cup cold water

1: In a medium-sized bowl, sift together the flour and salt.
2: Stir in the oil.
3: Stir in the water and knead the dough 3 or 4 times until moist.
4: Roll out the dough.
5: Place the crust in the pie plate.
6: Finish the edge.

Graham Cracker Crust

1½ cups Graham cracker crumbs
6 tablespoons melted butter
3 tablespoons date sugar
½ teaspoon ground cinnamon

1: Preheat oven to 350°F.
2: Prepare the crumbs by crushing Graham crackers in a blender or between two sheets of waxed paper with a rolling pin.
3: In a medium-sized bowl, blend the crumbs, butter, sweetener and cinnamon.
4: Press the mixture into the bottom and sides of a 9″ pie plate, spreading the mixture evenly in the plate.
5: Place another 9″ pie plate over the crust and press to smooth the crust and distribute it evenly over the sides and bottom of the pie plate.
6: Bake for 10 to 15 minutes.
7: Cool the crust. Add the filling.

Apple Pie

1 Double Whole Wheat Pie Crust
½ cup honey
½ teaspoon cinnamon
¼ teaspoon nutmeg
2 tablespoons pastry flour
8 to 10 McIntosh apples
2 or 3 pats butter (optional)

1: Preheat oven to 375°F.
2: Prepare the crust. Line the bottom of a 9" pie plate with one crust and set the other aside.
3: In a 1-cup liquid measuring cup, mix the honey, cinnamon, nutmeg and flour.
4: Wash, peel and core the apples. Slice enough apples to cover the bottom of the pie plate.
5: Pour ⅓ of the honey mixture over the apples.
6: Add another layer of sliced apples.
7: Pour in ⅓ more of the honey mixture.
8: Add one more layer of sliced apples.
9: Pour on remaining honey mixture.
10: Dot top with butter if desired.
11: Place the top crust on the pie.
12: Finish the edge of the crust and cut 4 or 5 slashes in the center for air vents.
13: Bake for 50 minutes to 1 hour until the crust is evenly browned and filling is bubbling.
14: Cool the pie thoroughly on a wire rack before cutting and serving with a metal spatula.

Blueberry Pie

1 Double Whole Wheat Pie Crust or 1 Single Whole Wheat
Crust and Crumb Topping (see below)
1 quart blueberries
⅓ to ½ cup honey
3 tablespoons tapioca
2 or 3 pats butter (optional)

1: Preheat oven to 375°F.
2: Prepare the crust. Line the bottom of a 9″ pie plate with one
crust and set the other aside. Or, make a single-crust pie and top
filling with Crumb Topping (recipe below).
3: In a medium-sized bowl, combine the berries, honey and
tapioca.
4: Pour the berry mixture into the pie crust.
5: Dot with butter if using a top crust. Cover with the top crust or
crumb topping.
6: Bake for 50 minutes to 1 hour, until the crust is evenly browned
and the filling is bubbling.
7: Cool pie thoroughly on a wire rack before cutting and serving.

Crumb Topping

⅓ cup oil or soft butter
1 cup rolled oats
½ cup flour
¼ to ⅓ cup honey

1: In a medium-sized bowl, blend together all the ingredients.
2: Spread the mixture evenly over the top of the blueberries.

Squash Pie

1 Single Whole Wheat Pie Crust
⅔ cup milk
1 tablespoon butter
2 cups mashed squash (any winter variety)
⅓ cup honey
¼ teaspoon sea salt
½ teaspoon cinnamon
¼ teaspoon nutmeg
¼ teaspoon pumpkin pie spice
2 eggs

1: Preheat oven to 375°F.
2: Prepare the crust. Line the bottom of a 9″ pie plate with the crust and finish the edges.
3: In a small saucepan, combine the milk and butter and place over medium heat to scald, heating to approximately 180°F. or until a ring of bubbles forms around the edge of the milk. Do not boil.
4: In a medium-sized bowl, combine the squash, honey, salt and spices.
5: Crack the eggs into a small bowl; dip a pastry brush into the egg white and brush the bottom of the pie crust, to prevent it from becoming soggy.
6: Beat the eggs and add to the squash mixture, stirring well.
7: Stir in the warm milk.
8: Pour the squash mixture into the pie crust.
9: Sprinkle the top of the pie with pumpkin pie spice.
10: Bake for 50 minutes to 1 hour, until the crust is evenly browned and the filling is firm.
11: Cool pie thoroughly on a wire rack before cutting and serving.

Carob Cream Pie

1 Single Whole Wheat Pie Crust or 1 Graham Cracker Crust
Carob Pudding (see recipe)
Sweetened Whipped Cream (see recipe)

1: Preheat oven to 400°F.
2: Prepare the crust and line a 9″ pie plate. Pierce the bottom and sides of the wheat crust with a fork and bake for 10 to 15 minutes, or until crisp. Cool crust before adding filling.
3: Fill the cooled crust with carob pudding.
4: Chill the pie for several hours or overnight.
5: Top the pie with sweetened whipped cream and chill again before serving. Cut with a hot, sharp knife. (Hold the knife under hot water to heat it and dry before using.)

Banana Cream Pie

1 Single Whole Wheat Pie Crust or 1 Graham Cracker Crust
Vanilla Pudding (see recipe)
2 to 3 bananas
Sweetened Whipped Cream (see recipe)

1: Preheat oven to 400°F.
2: Prepare the crust and line a 9″ pie plate. Pierce the bottom and sides of the wheat crust with a fork and bake for 10 to 15 minutes, or until crisp. Cool crust before adding the filling.
3: Slice enough bananas to fill the pie plate.
4: Pour the vanilla pudding over the bananas.
5: Chill the pie for several hours or overnight.
6: Top the pie with the sweetened whipped cream.
7: Chill before serving. Cut with a hot, sharp knife. (Hold the knife under hot water to heat it and dry before using.)

Peach Pie

1 Double Whole Wheat Pie Crust or 1 Single Whole Wheat
   Pie Crust and Crumb Topping (see Blueberry Pie)
3 pounds peaches
⅓ cup honey
3 tablespoons tapioca
½ teaspoon mace
2 or 3 pats butter

1: Preheat oven to 375°F.
2: Prepare the double crust or the single crust and crumb topping.
   Line the bottom of a 9″ pie plate with one crust and set the other
   aside.
3: Peel and slice the peaches into a large bowl.
4: Stir in the honey, tapioca and mace.
5: Pour the peach mixture into the pie crust.
6: Dot peaches with butter if using a top crust.
7: Cover pie with the top crust or crumb topping.
8: Bake for 50 minutes to 1 hour.
9: Cool pie thoroughly on a wire rack before cutting and serving.

Roll-Ups

1 Single Whole Wheat Pie Dough or pieces of leftover dough
¼ cup Raisins or adjusted to amount of dough
¼ cup Walnuts or adjusted to amount of dough
¼ cup Coconut or adjusted to amount of dough
Maple Syrup to moisten

1: Oil a baking sheet and preheat oven to 400°F.
2: Place the dough between two sheets of waxed paper and roll out into a rectangular shape. The dough should be approximately ⅜'' thick.
3: In a medium-sized bowl, combine the raisins, chopped nuts and coconut to sprinkle over the pie dough.
4: Add enough maple syrup to barely moisten the other ingredients.
5: Spread the mixture loosely over the dough.
6: Cut the dough into strips 1½'' wide.
7: Roll the strips of dough and filling up into spirals, cutting when 1'' in diameter.
8: Place the rolls, seam side down, on the baking sheet.
9: Bake for 10 to 15 minutes until browned.
10: Cool roll-ups on a wire rack.

Puddings and Desserts

How To Make Puddings

These puddings are cooked either entirely on top of the stove, or first on top and then baked in the oven. The puddings cooked entirely on top of the stove are thickened with arrowroot starch, also called arrowroot flour. It is ground from the tuberous roots of certain plants and has a greater nutritive value than cornstarch, the more commonly used thickener. Arrowroot makes a very thick pudding, also excellent for pie filling. These puddings are perishable; it is best to eat them within 24 hours after preparation. Chill and store the pudding in the refrigerator after cooking, otherwise it will separate and spoil.

For the baked puddings, the milk is first cooked on top of the stove and then combined with the remaining ingredients to be baked in the oven. The result is a delicious pudding just like grandmother used to make. Store these puddings in the refrigerator after cooling in the baking dish on the wire rack.

Vanilla Pudding

¼ cup honey or maple syrup
3 tablespoons arrowroot
½ teaspoon sea salt
1¾ cups milk
2 egg yolks
2 tablespoons butter
1 teaspoon vanilla

1: In a medium-sized saucepan, combine the honey, arrowroot and salt, stirring until the arrowroot is dissolved.
2: Stir in the milk.
3: Cook over medium heat, stirring constantly for 10 minutes, or until the mixture thickens and boils. Allow to boil for 1 minute.
4: In a 1-cup measuring cup, beat the egg yolks.
5: Remove the milk mixture from the heat and gradually stir half of it into the beaten egg yolks.
6: Add the egg mixture to the remaining milk mixture in the saucepan.
7: Return the pan to the heat and boil over medium heat for 1 minute.
8: Remove from the heat and stir in the butter and vanilla.
9: Beat the pudding with a wire whisk or egg beater to remove any lumps.
10: Pour into dessert dishes, cover and chill. Serve within 24 hours.

VARIATIONS:
Fold ⅓ cup toasted coconut, sliced bananas, berries, or other fruits into the finished pudding before chilling.

Use this pudding in a pie crust for Banana Cream Pie (see recipe).

Leftover egg whites? Try Coconut Puffs.

Carob Pudding

¼ cup honey
3 tablespoons arrowroot
½ teaspoon sea salt
¼ cup carob powder
2 cups milk
2 egg yolks
2 tablespoons butter
½ teaspoon vanilla
1 cup Sweetened Whipped Cream (see recipe)

1: In a medium-sized saucepan, combine the honey, arrowroot, salt, and carob and stir until evenly moist.
2: Gradually stir in the milk.
3: Cook over medium heat, stirring constantly for 10 minutes, or until the mixture thickens and boils. Allow to boil for 1 minute.
4: In a 1-cup measuring cup, beat the egg yolks.
5: Remove the milk mixture from the heat and stir half of it into the beaten egg yolks.
6: Add the egg mixture to the remaining milk mixture in the saucepan.
7: Return the pan to the heat and boil over medium heat for 1 minute.
8: Remove from the heat and stir in the butter and vanilla.
9: Beat the pudding with a wire whisk or egg beater to remove any lumps.
10: Pour into dessert dishes, cover and chill. Serve within 24 hours. Top with whipped cream (recipe below).

VARIATIONS:
Fold ¼ cup chopped walnuts, coconut or carob chips into the finished pudding before chilling.

Use this pudding as a filling for Carob Cream Pie.

Leftover egg whites? Try Coconut Puffs.

Tapioca Pudding

2 eggs, separated
1¾ cups milk
¼ cup maple syrup
2 tablespoons tapioca
¼ teaspoon sea salt
1 teaspoon vanilla

1: In a small saucepan, combine the egg yolks, milk, maple syrup, tapioca and salt.
2: Cook over medium heat, stirring constantly, until mixture thickens and boils.
3: Remove pan from the heat and allow to cool to room temperature; if not adequately cooled, the pudding will separate.
4: Stir in the vanilla.
5: Using an electric mixer, whip the egg whites in a medium-sized bowl until stiff.
6: Fold the cooled milk mixture into the egg whites.
7: Pour into dessert dishes, cover and chill before serving. Serve within 24 hours.

Rice Pudding

1½ cups milk
¼ cup butter
2½ cups cooked brown rice
½ cup raisins
1 egg
⅓ cup honey
½ teaspoon vanilla
¼ teaspoon nutmeg

1: Butter a 2-quart baking dish and preheat oven to 350°F.
2: Combine the milk and butter in a small saucepan and place over medium heat to scald, heating to approximately 180°F., or until a ring of bubbles forms around the edge of the milk. Do not boil.
3: In a medium-sized bowl, mix together the remaining ingredients.
4: Stir in the scalded milk.
5: Pour the mixture into the baking dish.
6: Place the dish in a pan filled 1″ deep with hot water and place in the oven.
7: Bake for 2 hours.
8: Cool before serving. Store in the refrigerator.

Bread Pudding SERVES 8

1½ cups milk
¼ cup butter
3 cups whole wheat bread cubes
½ cup honey
½ cup raisins
2 eggs
½ teaspoon vanilla
¼ teaspoon sea salt
¾ teaspoon cinnamon
¼ teaspoon nutmeg

1: Butter a 2-quart baking dish and preheat oven to 350°F.
2: In a small saucepan, combine the milk and butter and place over medium heat to scald, heating to approximately 180°F., or until a ring of bubbles forms around the edge of the milk. Do not boil.
3: In a medium-sized bowl, combine the remaining ingredients.
4: Stir in the scalded milk.
5: Pour the mixture into the baking dish.
6: Place the dish in a pan filled 1" deep with hot water and place in the oven.
7: Bake for 40 minutes.
8: Cool before serving.

Indian Pudding

SERVES 8

3⅔ cups milk
⅔ cup molasses
⅓ cup honey
⅔ cup corn meal
1 teaspoon sea salt
¾ teaspoon cinnamon
¾ teaspoon nutmeg
¼ cup butter

1: Butter a 2-quart baking dish and preheat oven to 300°F.
2: In a large saucepan, combine 2⅔ cups of the milk, the molasses and honey and place over medium-low heat.
3: In a medium-sized bowl, combine the corn meal, salt and spices.
4: Gradually stir the corn meal mixture into the hot liquid.
5: Add the butter.
6: Cook over medium-low heat, stirring frequently, for approximately 10 minutes until the mixture thickens.
7: Pour into the baking dish.
8: Pour the remaining cup of milk over the pudding; do not stir.
9: Bake for 3 hours.
10: Serve warm or cool with cream or honey-sweetened ice cream.

Ambrosia SERVES 6 TO 8

1 large (16-ounce) can unsweetened fruit cocktail
1 small (8-ounce) can unsweetened pineapple chunks
2 bananas, sliced
½ cup coconut
1 cup whipping cream
2 tablespoons honey
½ teaspoon vanilla

1: Drain the canned fruits.
2: In a medium-sized bowl, combine the fruit cocktail, pineapple, bananas and coconut.
3: Using an electric mixer, whip the cream in a large bowl until it begins to stiffen.
4: Add the honey and vanilla and beat with the mixer until stiff.
5: Fold the fruit into the whipped cream.
6: Chill for 3 to 4 hours or overnight before serving.

Apple Crisp SERVES 6 TO 8

8 medium apples
¼ cup honey
1½ tablespoons tapioca

1: Preheat oven to 350°F.
2: Wash, peel, and slice the apples into a mixing bowl.
3: Add the honey and tapioca and stir well.
4: Place the apple mixture in a 2-quart buttered baking dish.
5: Top with Granola or Oat Topping (see recipes).
6: Bake for 25 minutes.

VARIATION:
Substitute peeled and sliced peaches for the apples.

Maple-Walnut Granola

MAKES 8 CUPS

4 cups rolled oats
1 cup wheat germ
1 cup sesame seeds
1 cup coconut
1 cup chopped or broken walnuts
¼ cup oil
½ cup maple syrup
¼ cup honey

1: Preheat oven to 250°F.
2: In a large mixing bowl, combine the oats, wheat germ, seeds, coconut and nuts.
3: Add the oil and stir until evenly distributed.
4: Pour in the maple syrup, stirring well.
5: Add the honey and mix well until evenly moistened and the mixture is crumbly and sticky.
6: Spread the mixture in a large shallow pan such as the bottom of an oven broiler pan.
7: Bake for 1½ hours, stirring every 15 minutes for even browning, until the mixture is golden brown and dry.
8: Cool thoroughly and store in airtight containers.

VARIATIONS:
Use granola in Apple Crisp or Granola Cookies (see recipes).

Granola Topping

1½ cups Maple-Walnut Granola (see recipe)
¼ cup soft butter

1: In a small bowl, mix the granola and butter until crumbly.

Oat Topping

1½ cups rolled oats
¼ cup butter
¼ cup honey
½ teaspoon cinnamon
¼ teaspoon nutmeg
¼ cup chopped walnuts

1: In a small bowl, combine all the ingredients and mix until crumbly.

Applesauce

MAKES ½ GALLON

3 pounds apples
½ cup water
Vanilla to taste
Cinnamon to taste
Nutmeg to taste

1: Wash the apples and cut into quarters, unpeeled. The peels add flavor and color. (If a quicker sauce is desired, peel and seed apples.)
2: Place the apples in a large pot.
3: Add the water.
4: Cook over medium heat, stirring often, for 1 to 2 hours.
5: When apples have reached desired consistency, remove from heat and cool.
6: Strain the apples in a fruit strainer or a colander over a large bowl, pushing the apples through the colander with a spatula; discard the skins.
7: Add vanilla, cinnamon and nutmeg to taste. Do not over-spice; the flavor will increase as the sauce cools.
8: Cool before serving. Store in an airtight container in the refrigerator or freeze for later use.

Baked Apples

SERVES 4

4 apples
1 teaspoon butter
4 teaspoons honey
Sprinkle of cinnamon

1: Preheat oven to 375°F.
2: Wash and core the apples.
3: Place the apples in a baking pan.
   Cover the bottom of the pan with ¼" water.
4: Place ¼ teaspoon of butter, 1 teaspoon of honey and a sprinkle of cinnamon into the center of each apple.
5: Bake for 45 minutes or until apples can be easily pierced with a fork.

Sweetened Whipped Cream   MAKES 2 CUPS

1 cup heavy cream
2 tablespoons honey
½ teaspoon vanilla

1: Chill a medium-sized bowl and 2 electric mixer beaters in the refrigerator for ½ hour.
2: Place the cream in the chilled bowl and whip, using the chilled beaters.
3: As the cream begins to stiffen, add the honey in a slow stream, continuing to beat.
4: Add the vanilla and beat with the electric mixer until the cream is stiff and forms peaks.
5: Chill and serve over your favorite dessert. Store in an airtight container in the refrigerator; stir until smooth before use.

Unyeasted Breads

How To Make Unyeasted Breads

The most common leavening agents used in baking are baking powder, baking soda and yeast. All of these produce carbon dioxide bubbles in the batter or dough, which cause the bread to rise. Baking powder and baking soda do not require time for rising before baking, as yeast breads do. Check the ingredients when purchasing baking powders, as most commercial brands are made with aluminum compounds and refined salt. Rumford, Royal and Walnut Acres are available brands which do not use aluminum, or you can make your own. Here are two recipes:

Baking Powder No. 1

2 teaspoons cream of tartar
1 teaspoon bicarbonate of soda
2 teaspoons arrowroot

Combine all the ingredients. Use in the same amounts as commercial baking powders.

Baking Powder No. 2

2 teaspoons cream of tartar
1 teaspoon bicarbonate of soda
½ teaspoon sea salt

Combine all the ingredients. Use 3½ teaspoons for each cup of flour. Use fresh; do not store.

Baking powder and soda are activated when moistened, so place the bread in the oven as soon as possible after adding the leavening to the liquid ingredients. To save time after mixing, oil the pan before mixing the batter. It is also important to preheat the oven. For the bread to rise properly, it must be hit with high heat instantly upon being placed in the oven. This is particularly important to insure that your whole wheat breads will be as light and finely textured as possible. If your muffins come out with flat tops, most likely the oven was not hot enough when you put them in.

Whole Wheat Muffins

MAKES 1 DOZEN

¼ cup oil
¼ cup honey
1½ cups milk
1 egg
½ teaspoon sea salt
2 teaspoons baking powder
2 cups whole wheat flour

1: Oil a 12-cup muffin tin and preheat the oven to 400°F.
2: In a medium-sized bowl, combine the oil, honey and milk.
3: Beat the egg and add to the oil mixture, stirring well.
4: Stir in the salt, baking powder and 1 cup of the flour.
5: Add the remaining cup of flour and stir until batter is evenly moist.
6: Pour the batter into the muffin tin, filling each cup to the top. Fill any empty cups with water to prevent the muffin tin from losing shape while baking.
7: Bake for 20 minutes.
8: Place the muffin tin on a wire rack and cool for 5 to 10 minutes. Carefully loosen and remove the muffins from the tin.

VARIATIONS:
Fold 1 cup blueberries, or ½ cup nuts, dried fruit or seeds into the finished batter.

Bran Muffins

MAKES 1 DOZEN

¼ cup oil
¼ cup molasses
1½ cups milk
1 egg
½ teaspoon sea salt
1½ teaspoons baking powder
½ teaspoon baking soda
1 cup bran flakes
1 cup whole wheat flour
½ cup raisins

1: Oil a 12-cup muffin tin and preheat oven to 400°F.
2: In a medium-sized bowl, combine the oil, molasses and milk.
3: In a 1-cup liquid measuring cup, beat the egg. Add to the oil mixture, stirring well.
4: Stir in the salt, baking powder, baking soda and bran.
5: Add the flour and stir until batter is evenly moist.
6: Fold in the raisins.
7: Pour the batter into the muffin tin, filling the cups to the top.
8: Bake for 20 minutes.
9: Place the muffin tin on a wire rack and cool for 5 to 10 minutes. Carefully loosen and remove the muffins from the tin.

Corn Bread   MAKES 16 SQUARES

½ cup whole wheat flour
1½ cups corn meal
1 teaspoon sea salt
3 teaspoons baking powder
3 eggs
1 cup milk
1 tablespoon honey
¼ cup light cream
⅓ cup melted butter

1: Oil a 9″ x 9″ pan and preheat oven to 400°F.
2: Combine the dry ingredients in a medium-sized bowl.
3: Add the eggs, milk and honey and stir well.
4: Stir in the cream.
5: Add the butter, blending well.
6: Spread the batter into the pan.
7: Bake for 15 to 20 minutes.
8: Serve hot.

Banana Bread

MAKES 2 LOAVES

½ cup oil
½ cup honey
1 teaspoon vanilla
2 eggs
3 ripe bananas
1½ teaspoons baking soda
1 teaspoon sea salt
1¾ cups whole wheat flour
1 cup chopped walnuts

1: Oil two 7⅞" x 3⅞" loaf pans and preheat oven to 375°F.
2: In a medium-sized bowl, combine the oil, honey and vanilla.
3: Beat the eggs and add to the oil mixture, stirring well.
4: In a separate bowl, mash the bananas and add to the honey mixture.
5: Add the soda, salt and half of the flour and blend until batter is evenly moist.
6: Mix in the remaining flour.
7: Fold in the nuts.
8: Divide the batter in half and spread into the two loaf pans.
9: Bake for 1 hour.
10: Remove the loaves from the pans and allow to cool on a wire rack.

Baking Powder Biscuits

MAKES 2 DOZEN

2 cups whole wheat flour
1 teaspoon sea salt
3 teaspoons baking powder
⅓ cup soft butter
1 cup milk

1: Preheat oven to 425°F.
2: In a medium-sized bowl, combine the flour, salt and baking powder.
3: Using a fork, cut the butter into the flour mixture until the butter is evenly distributed and forms a coarse meal.
4: Stir in enough of the milk to just moisten the flour.
5: Knead the dough slightly to make the flour evenly moist. The result should be a soft dough that is not too dry. More flour will be worked in during the rolling out and cutting.
6: Place the dough on a lightly floured board and roll out until ½" to ⅝" thick.
7: Using the rim of a glass, dipped in flour to prevent sticking, cut the dough into round biscuits.
8: Lift the biscuits onto an ungreased baking sheet. Re-knead the remaining scraps of dough and roll out again, making as many biscuits as possible.
9: Bake for 10 to 12 minutes.

Date-Nut Bread

MAKES 2 LOAVES

1 cup plain yoghurt
1 egg
2 tablespoons oil
½ cup honey
1 teaspoon baking soda
2 cups whole wheat flour
1 to 2 cups chopped dates
1 cup chopped walnuts

1: Oil two 7⅞" x 3⅞" loaf pans and preheat oven to 350°F.
2: In a medium-sized bowl, combine the yoghurt, egg, oil and honey.
3: Add the soda and 1 cup of the flour and stir until the batter is evenly moist.
4: Stir in the dates and nuts.
5: Add the remaining cup of flour and mix until moist.
6: Divide the batter in half and spread into the two loaf pans.
7: Bake for 40 minutes.
8: Remove the loaves from the pans and allow to cool on a wire rack.

VARIATION:
Cranberry-Nut Bread: Substitute 1 cup of fresh cranberries for the dates and prepare as above.

Steamed Bread MAKES 3 LOAVES

2 cups corn meal
2 cups rye flour
1 cup whole wheat flour
1 cup bran flakes
1 teaspoon sea salt
1 teaspoon cinnamon
2 teaspoons baking powder
1 cup honey
3 cups milk
1 cup chopped dates
1 cup chopped walnuts

1: Oil three 1-pound coffee cans.
2: Combine the dry ingredients in a large bowl and stir well.
3: Add the honey and half of the milk, mixing well.
4: Add the remaining milk and stir until well blended.
5: Fold in the dates and nuts.
6: Pour 2½ cups of the batter into each coffee can.
7: Cover the cans tightly with aluminum foil.
8: Place the cans on top of cookie cutters or a wire rack or trivet in the bottom of a large pot.
9: Fill the pot with 2" to 3" of hot water, or enough to cover the bottoms of the cans.
10: Cover the pot, bring the water to a boil, and steam for 2 hours. Check the water level occasionally, adding water as needed.
11: After steaming, remove the bread from the cans and allow to cool on a wire rack.
12: Serve plain or toasted. This bread is very rich, so cut into thin slices.

Chapati

2 cups whole wheat flour
½ teaspoon salt
¾ to 1 cup water

1: In a medium-sized bowl, combine the flour and salt.
2: Add enough of the water to moisten all of the flour and form a stiff dough.
3: Place the dough on a lightly-floured board and knead for 1 to 2 minutes, until smooth and dry.
4: Return the dough to the bowl and cover with a dry towel. Let stand for 30 minutes.
5: Break off pieces of dough large enough to make 1½" balls.
6: Using a floured rolling pin roll each ball out on a lightly floured board until it is very thin and approximately 8" in diameter.
7: Place a lightly oiled skillet over medium heat; add the chapati and cook for approximately 1 minute, until the edge of the bread begins to curl up. Flip the bread over and cook the other side. The bread is done when it is firm, but still flexible. Over-cooking will make the bread too brittle.
8: Fill with your favorite sandwich spread and fold over or roll up or cool and store in an airtight container for later use.

Pancakes

¼ cup oil
1 tablespoon honey
2 eggs
1 cup milk
1½ teaspoons baking powder
½ teaspoon sea salt
1½ cups pastry flour

1: In a medium-sized bowl, combine the oil, honey and eggs.
2: Stir in the milk.
3: Add the baking powder, salt, and 1 cup of the flour, stirring well.
4: Gradually add enough of the remaining flour to make a batter that pours evenly, but is not too runny.
5: Place an oiled skillet or grill over high heat until drops of water dance on it. Reduce heat to medium; pour batter from a measuring cup onto the skillet in small circles.
6: Cook until bubbles appear on the top of each pancake; turn before the bubbles break.
7: Brown the second side, cooking the middle thoroughly.
8: Serve hot with butter and maple syrup, honey or fruit butter.

Waffles

1½ cups pastry flour
2 teaspoons baking powder
½ teaspoon sea salt
2 eggs, separated
1 tablespoon honey
4 tablespoons oil
1 to 1½ cups milk

1: Combine the dry ingredients in a medium-sized bowl.
2: Add the egg yolks, honey, oil and milk, stirring until the flour is evenly moist.
3: In a separate bowl, using an electric mixer, whip the egg whites until stiff.
4: Gently fold the egg whites into the batter.
5: Oil and heat a waffle iron; pour in the batter, filling the iron two-thirds full.
6: Close the waffle iron and cook until iron is no longer steaming.
7: Cook all of the batter and serve hot with butter and maple syrup, honey or fruit butters.

Yeasted Breads

How To Make Yeasted Bread

Making bread does not need to be difficult. It just takes a lot of time and a little muscle—time to allow the bread to rise, and muscle for kneading the dough. The kneading can be done a little at a time as long as the bread is not allowed to rise until enough flour has been kneaded in. With a little practice you won't want anything but your own home-baked breads.

To Prepare the Dough:
1: Read the whole recipe.
2: Work in an area free from drafts.
3: In a large mixing bowl, dissolve the yeast in warm water by sprinkling the yeast over the surface of the water and allowing it to stand, without stirring, for 5 to 10 minutes. These recipes call for dry yeast which requires a water temperature of 105°F. to 115°F. If using compressed yeast, water temperature should be 80°F. Substitute 1 cake compressed yeast for every 2 tablespoons dry yeast. Store yeast in the refrigerator.
4: Stir in the remaining water, if any.
5: Add the salt, oil and sweetener, stirring well.
6: Add 3 cups of the flour and stir until the mixture is well blended and there are no lumps.
7: Gradually add the remaining flour, 1 cup at a time, stirring well after each addition, until it is too thick to stir. Fold in more of the flour until the dough forms one firm mass and pulls away from the sides of the bowl. The dough should be moist, but without many wet and stringy spots. However, it is better to have dough that is too wet rather than too dry, as you can always knead in a little more flour, but it is difficult to get a smooth dough once it is too dry.
8: Lightly flour a bread board or counter.
9: Using a rubber spatula, scrape all of the dough and any loose flour from the bowl onto the floured board.
10: Sprinkle flour over the surface of the dough and on your hands. Keep sprinkling flour over the board, the dough, and your hands as you knead, to prevent sticking. If the dough sticks to

your hands, rub them together and knead the pieces that roll off your hands back into the dough.

11: To begin kneading, fold a handful of the dough toward the center of the ball.

12: Press from the center, along the seam, down and away from yourself, pressing firmly with the heel of the hand.

13: Turn the dough, fold in another handful of dough and press together along the seam. Continue turning, folding and pressing the dough for 10 to 20 minutes, depending on the amount of flour that has to be kneaded in.

The dough is ready when:
—the surface is dry to the touch
—there are no cracks in the surface
—the seam is not sticky
—the dough springs back when poked

14: Place the dough, seam side down, back into the unwashed mixing bowl. Cover the bowl with a towel moistened with hot water.

15: Place the bowl in a warm place (75–80°F.), free from drafts (such as on top of the refrigerator).

16: Clean up the kneading area.

17: Allow the dough to rise for 1 to 2 hours until double in bulk. The surface of the dough should be smooth, without cracks and bubbles which result when it has risen too much. Test the dough by poking with a finger. If it leaves a hole, the dough has risen enough. If the dough does rise too much, knead longer before forming into loaves. Do not allow the loaves to rise too high or the bread will be crumbly and fall apart when sliced.

18: Using a rubber spatula, scrape the dough out of the bowl onto a lightly floured board.

19: Form the dough into a rectangular shape. The flour on the board and a little on your hands should be enough to handle the dough without sticking.

To Form the Loaves

20: Cut the dough into 3 equal portions; each portion will weigh about 1 pound.

21: Oil three 7⅞" x 3⅞" loaf pans, or make 2 larger loaves using

8½″ x 4½″ loaf pans. The smaller pan gives a taller loaf, and a smaller slice.

22: Knead one of the portions of dough 5 to 10 times to smooth out the surface; shape it into a triangle.

23: Place the triangle of dough onto a floured board, with the point of the triangle toward you.

24: Roll the dough out with a floured rolling pin, adding flour to the rolling pin and the bread board as needed, to prevent sticking. Roll the dough out until the larger end is the length of the loaf pan, approximately ½″ thick, so that the loaf will reach the ends of the pan and the bread will rise up, not out.

25: Beginning with the narrow end, roll the dough up, pressing firmly to avoid spaces between layers.

26: Place the rolled-up dough into the oiled pan with the seam side down, folding any excess dough under the ends.

27: Form the other 2 loaves the same way as the first and place in the pans.

28: Allow the dough to rise in a warm place, uncovered, for 45 minutes to 1 hour, until double in bulk. The rounded top of the loaf will appear above the top of the pan when it has risen enough; it will rise a little more during baking.

To Bake and Store

29: Handle the risen loaves gently; they fall easily. Place the loaves in a preheated oven and bake. Different baking temperatures produce different results. Bake at 350°F. for 1 hour for a soft moist loaf. Bake at 400°F. for 20 to 30 minutes for a firmer, drier loaf. The bread is done if the loaf sounds hollow when tapped with a finger. If not done, bake for a few minutes more.

30: Carefully remove the loaves from the pans. Wipe the entire crust of each loaf with a cold, wet cloth to set the crust.

31: Allow the bread to cool completely on wire racks for several hours before wrapping it in plastic bags or a linen towel for storage. The bread will store well in the refrigerator, or it may be frozen for later use. After thawing, store in the refrigerator, as frozen foods lose their freshness more quickly.

Whole Wheat Bread

3 cups warm water
1 tablespoon dry yeast
1 tablespoon sea salt
2 tablespoons oil
2 tablespoons honey
6 to 8 cups whole wheat flour

1: In a large bowl, dissolve the yeast in ½ cup of the warm water.
2: Add the remaining warm water, stirring well.
3: Mix in the salt, oil and honey.
4: Add 3 cups of the flour; stir until smooth and evenly moistened.
5: Add the remaining flour, 1 cup at a time, stirring after each addition, until the dough is too thick to stir. Fold in more of the flour until the dough forms one firm mass and pulls away from the sides of the bowl, but is still moist.
6: Scrape the dough from the bowl onto a lightly floured board.
7: Knead the dough for 10 to 20 minutes until it is smooth and elastic.
8: Return the dough to the bowl and cover with a warm, moist towel.
9: Place the dough in a warm place, free from drafts, and allow to rise until double in bulk (approximately 1 to 2 hours).
10: Scrape the dough out of the bowl onto a lightly floured board.
11: Oil three 7⅞″ x 3⅜″ loaf pans, or two 8½″ x 4½″ loaf pans.
12: Cut the dough into 2 or 3 equal portions, depending on the number of loaves desired.
13: Form each portion into a loaf and place in one of the loaf pans.
14: Allow the loaves to rise, uncovered, for approximately 45 minutes, until double in bulk.
15: Preheat oven to 350°F. and bake the loaves for 1 hour; for a firmer loaf, bake at 400°F. for 20 to 30 minutes.
16: Carefully remove the loaves from the pans; wipe the entire crust of each loaf with a cold, wet cloth.
17: Cool the loaves thoroughly on wire racks before storing in plastic bags.

Raisin Bread

3½ cups warm water
1 tablespoon dry yeast
1 tablespoon sea salt
1 tablespoon cinnamon
½ teaspoon ground ginger
2 tablespoons oil
2 tablespoons molasses
1½ cups raisins
9 to 10 cups whole wheat flour

1: In a large bowl, dissolve the yeast in the warm water.
2: Add the salt, cinnamon and ginger and stir well.
3: Stir in the oil, molasses and raisins.
4: Add 4 cups of the flour and stir until well blended.
5: Add the remaining flour, 1 cup at a time, stirring well after each addition until the dough is too thick to stir. Fold in more of the flour until the dough forms one firm mass and pulls away from the sides of the bowl, but is still moist.
6: Scrape the dough from the bowl onto a lightly floured board.
7: Knead the dough for 10 to 20 minutes until smooth and elastic.
8: Cut the dough into 2 or 3 equal portions, depending on the number of loaves desired.
9: Form the portions into loaves and place them in three oiled 7⅞" x 3⅞" loaf pans, or two 8½" x 4½" loaf pans.
10: Allow the bread to rise in the pans, uncovered, for 45 minutes to 1 hour until double in bulk. This bread only rises once.
11: Preheat oven to 350°F. Bake the loaves for 50 minutes to 1 hour, until brown and hollow sounding when tapped.
12: Carefully remove the loaves from the pans. Wipe the entire crust of the loaves with a cold, wet towel.
13: Cool the loaves thoroughly on wire racks before storing in plastic bags.

Cheese Bread

1¾ cups milk
1 tablespoon sea salt
4 tablespoons oil
2 tablespoons honey
½ cup warm water
2 tablespoons dry yeast
5 to 7 cups whole wheat flour
6 to 8 ounces grated sharp cheese
1 egg white
Sprinkle of sesame seeds

1: Place the milk in a saucepan and scald over medium heat, heating to approximately 180°F., or until a ring of bubbles forms around the edge of the milk. Do not boil.
2: Pour the scalded milk into a large mixing bowl.
3: Add the salt, oil and honey and stir well. Allow the mixture to cool.
4: In a small bowl, dissolve the yeast in the warm water.
5: When the milk mixture has cooled to warm, stir in the yeast.
6: Add 2 cups of the flour and stir until smooth.
7: Add the cheese and mix until well blended.
8: Add the remaining flour, 1 cup at a time, stirring after each addition, until the dough is too thick to stir. Fold in more flour until the dough forms a firm mass and pulls away from the sides of the bowl, but is still moist.
9: Scrape the dough from the bowl onto a lightly floured board.
10: Knead the dough for 10 to 20 minutes until dry and elastic. There may be some cracks in the surface from the cheese; these will smooth out during rising and baking.
11: Return the dough to the bowl and cover with a warm, moist towel.
12: Allow the dough to rise in a warm place, free from drafts, for 1 to 2 hours, until double in bulk.
13: Scrape the dough out of the bowl onto a lightly floured board.
14: Cut the dough into 2 or 3 equal portions, depending on the number of loaves desired.

15: Form the portions into loaves and place in three oiled 7⅞'' x 3⅞'' loaf pans, or two 8½'' x 4½'' loaf pans.

16: Allow the loaves to rise in the pans for ½ hour. Brush the top of each loaf with egg white diluted with a little water; sprinkle with sesame seeds.

17: Allow the loaves to rise for approximately 15 minutes more, until double in bulk.

18: Preheat oven to 350°F. Bake the loaves for 50 minutes to 1 hour until evenly browned and hollow sounding when tapped.

19: Carefully remove the loaves from the pans and allow to cool thoroughly on wire racks. (Do not wipe the loaves with cold water as that would wipe off the sesame seeds.)

Rye Bread

2 cups milk
1 tablespoon sea salt
2 tablespoons oil
1 tablespoon honey
2 tablespoons dry yeast
5 to 6 cups rye flour
1 tablespoon caraway seeds

1: Place the milk in a saucepan and scald over medium heat, heating to approximately 180°F., or until a ring of bubbles forms around the edge of the milk. Transfer to a large bowl and allow to cool.

2: Stir in the salt, oil and honey.

3: When the milk mixture has cooled to warm (approximately 110°F.), sprinkle in the yeast and allow it to dissolve.

4: Stir in 2 cups of the rye flour.

5: Cover the bowl with a warm, moist towel. Allow this mixture (called a sponge) to rise in a warm place, free from drafts, for 1 hour.

6: Stir in the seeds.

7: Add 3 cups of the remaining flour, 1 cup at a time, stirring and folding in after each addition.

8: Cover the dough with a warm, moist towel and allow to rise for approximately 2 hours.

9: Divide the dough in half. Knead in a little more flour while forming each half into a round or oval loaf.

10: Oil a baking sheet and dust with corn meal; place the loaves on the sheet.

11: Using a sharp knife, cut 3 or 4 slits across the top of each loaf.

12: Allow the loaves to rise for 2 hours.

13: Preheat oven to 350°F. Bake the loaves for 1 hour.

14: Wipe the loaves with a cold, wet towel and allow to cool thoroughly on wire racks.

Bibliography

Albright, Nancy. *The Rodale Cookbook*. Emmaus, Pa.: Rodale Press, 1976.

Beard, James. *James Beard's American Cookery*. Boston: Little, Brown and Co., 1972.

Betty Crocker's Cookbook. New York: McGraw Hill Book Co., 1961.

Brown, Edith and Sam. *Cooking Creatively with Natural Foods*. New York: Hawthorn Books, Inc., 1972.

Brown, Edward Espe. *Tassajara Bread Book*. Berkeley, Calif.: Shambhala, 1974.

Davis, Adelle. *Let's Eat Right to Keep Fit*. New York: Signet, 1970.

Dworkin, Stan and Floss. *The Good Goodies*. Emmaus, Pa.: Rodale Press, 1974.

Friedlander, Barbara. *Cookbook for the New Age: Earth Water Fire Air*. London: Collier Macmillan Publishers, 1973.

Hewitt, Jean. *The New York Times Heritage Cookbook*. New York: G.P. Putnam's Sons, 1972.

Hunter, Beatrice Trum. *The Natural Foods Cookbook*. New York: Pyramid Books, 1974.

Kloss, Jethro. *The Back to Eden Cookbook*. Santa Barbara, Calif.: Lifeline Books, 1974.

Rombauer, Irma S. and Becker, Marion Rombauer. *Joy of Cooking*. Indianapolis, Ind.: Bobbs-Merrill Co., 1972.

Sandler, Sandra and Bruce. *Home Bakebook of Natural Breads and Goodies*. Harrisburg, Pa.: Stackpole Books, 1972.

Stoner, Carol H. *Stocking Up*. Emmaus, Pa.: Rodale Press, 1975.

Talking Food Company. *Fiber*. Charlestown, Mass.: 1977.

Talking Food Company. *Sugar and How It Got That Way*. Charlestown, Mass.: 1977.

Talking Food Company. *More on Sugar and How It Got That Way*. Charlestown, Mass.: 1977.

Talking Food Company. *Our Daily Flour*. Charlestown, Mass.: 1977.

Talking Food Company. *Remedial Sweeteners*. Charlestown, Mass.: 1977.

Talking Food Company. *Vegetable Oil: The Unsaturated Facts*. Charlestown, Mass.: 1977.

Watt, Bernice K. and Merrill, Annabell L. *Composition of Foods*. Washington: United States Department of Agriculture, 1963.

Index

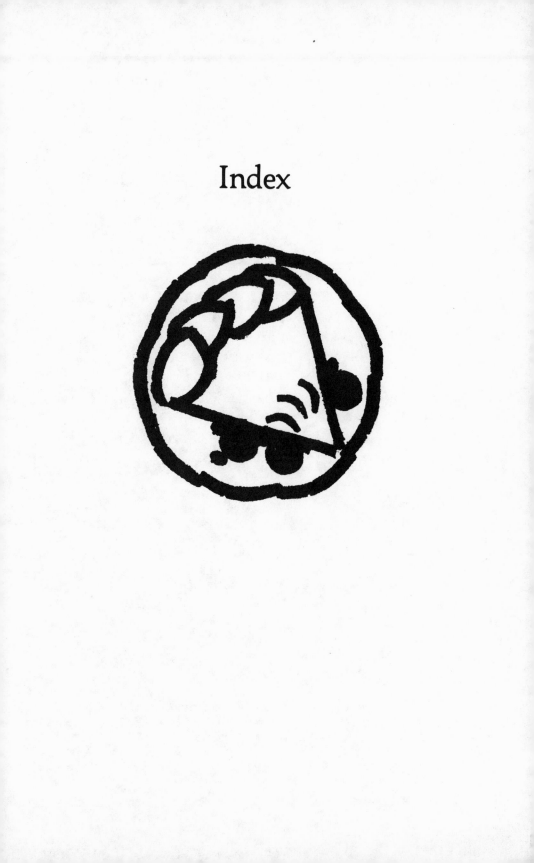

A